COLLINS HANDGUIDE TO THE

BIRDS

OF BRITAIN AND EUROPE

Painted by Hermann Heinzel

Text by Martin Woodcock

Collins St James's Place, London

William Collins Sons & Co Ltd
London · Glasgow · Sydney · Auckland
Toronto · Johannesburg

First published 1978

© in the text Martin Woodcock 1978

© in the illustrations Hermann Heinzel 1978

ISBN Hardback edition 0 00 219407 4

ISBN Paperback edition 0 00 219445 7

Colour reproduction by Adroit Photo Litho Ltd, Birmingham

Filmsetting by Jolly & Barber Ltd, Rugby

Printed and bound by
Wm Collins Sons & Co Ltd, Glasgow

Contents

The birds shown below are representatives of the principal families of British birds. They are shown in breeding (ie summer) plumage: remember that females, juveniles, and birds in their winter plumage out of the breeding season are often less brightly coloured or conspicuously marked. Under each illustration is a reference to the pages on which that group is described and illustrated.

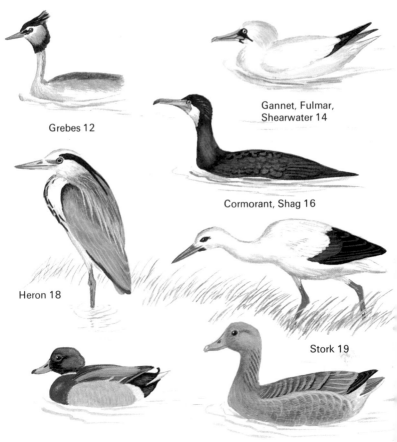

Grebes 12

Gannet, Fulmar, Shearwater 14

Cormorant, Shag 16

Heron 18

Stork 19

Swans, Geese & Ducks 20–24

Gamebirds 31

Coot & Moorhen 32

Birds of prey 26

Waders 34–38

Lapwing 34

Gulls 40–42

Terns 44

Auks 46

Pigeons & Doves 48–50

Kingfisher 53

Cuckoo 52

Hoopoe 53

Owls 54

Woodpeckers 56

Swift 59

Swallow 59

Larks &
Pipits 60

Wagtails 63

Warblers
64–66

Flycatchers 68

Wren 78

Robin & Redstarts
70

Nightingale 72

Thrushes &
Blackbird 73–74

Tits 77–78

Nuthatch,
Tree-creeper 79

Buntings 81

Finches & Sparrows 82–86

Starling 89

Oriole 88

Crows
90–92

Introduction

This book is meant as a simple introduction to the birds of the British Isles and western Europe, and as a lightweight guide to identifying the commonest or most conspicuous of them. It does not attempt to cover every species recorded — later you can move on to one of the more elaborate comprehensive guides, such as Hermann Heinzel's *Birds of Britain and Europe* or the Peterson *Field Guide* — because to start with it is more important, and more fun, to learn all we can about the birds we can expect to see in daily life, before bothering about rarities.

Britain is fortunate in having a rich and varied population of birds. Officially, over 450 species (as distinct kinds of plants and animals are called) have been recorded here. But this includes those that come infrequently, in very small numbers, or to few localities; many of them lost wanderers from Asia or America. Generally speaking about 200 species are plentiful here — some of them very widespread, others to be seen only in the right place and at the right time.

Most of the birds in this book are also common in western Europe; a few such as the Crested Lark, White Stork and Hoopoe, are far more familiar on the Continent than here. Some of our best-known birds like the Robin, Hedge Sparrow and Green Woodpecker are hardly found outside Europe as breeding species, but others like the Wren spread far across Asia and North America, while the Barn Owl is found all over the world.

No bird is found *only* in Britain, but several resident species (ie those which stay all year round) have as a result of their long isolation from their relatives on the Continent developed features that mark them out as slightly different. For example, our Pied Wagtail (p. 62) can be quite easily told, at least in summer, from its continental counterpart the White Wagtail; although biologically they remain the same species and may breed with each other.

WHERE THE BIRDS LIVE. Although they are so mobile, most birds are adapted to living in certain surroundings. Some species are more particular than others, but all are influenced by such factors as the availability of the food they need, nesting sites, cover and protection, or even songposts. A convenient name for a bird's typical surroundings is its "habitat". Different types of habitat in Britain include, for example, marshes, moor-

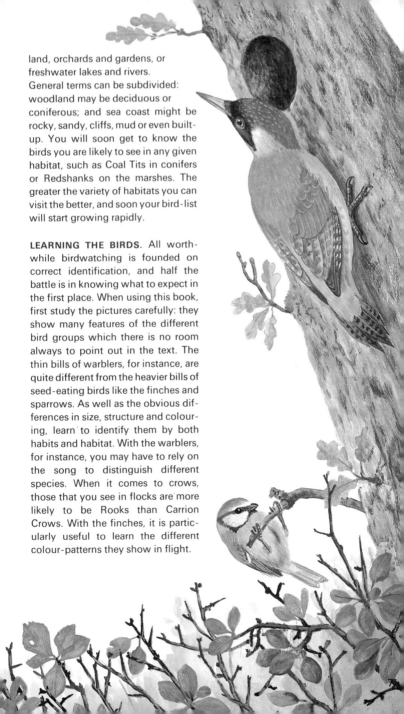

land, orchards and gardens, or freshwater lakes and rivers.

General terms can be subdivided: woodland may be deciduous or coniferous; and sea coast might be rocky, sandy, cliffs, mud or even built-up. You will soon get to know the birds you are likely to see in any given habitat, such as Coal Tits in conifers or Redshanks on the marshes. The greater the variety of habitats you can visit the better, and soon your bird-list will start growing rapidly.

LEARNING THE BIRDS. All worthwhile birdwatching is founded on correct identification, and half the battle is in knowing what to expect in the first place. When using this book, first study the pictures carefully: they show many features of the different bird groups which there is no room always to point out in the text. The thin bills of warblers, for instance, are quite different from the heavier bills of seed-eating birds like the finches and sparrows. As well as the obvious differences in size, structure and colouring, learn to identify them by both habits and habitat. With the warblers, for instance, you may have to rely on the song to distinguish different species. When it comes to crows, those that you see in flocks are more likely to be Rooks than Carrion Crows. With the finches, it is particularly useful to learn the different colour-patterns they show in flight.

SONG. Early in the year, the flocks of tits, finches, thrushes and others which have fed together through the fields and hedgerows all winter show signs of breaking up. Some males will posture or utter a short snatch of song before resuming their feeding, or indulge in aerial chases. Further south, in Africa and round the Mediterranean, our summer visitors the Cuckoo, Swallow and many others, start a gradual movement which gathers pace as spring moves northwards across Europe. One day we hear the mechanical ticking of the Chiffchaff as it hunts through the pussy-willows for insects: the first of the migrants adding his voice to the resident thrushes, robins, tits and sparrows which have been singing on and off for several weeks. Song now becomes a dominant feature of the bird world as the cocks establish their territories, singing to attract the attention of females and to warn off rivals. Some species like Nightingales and Garden Warblers like to sing from perches in thick cover, while Yellowhammers and the thrushes often sing from exposed perches; most birds have regular individual song-posts around their territory. Birds which nest in open country tend to sing in flight – Skylarks, Lapwings and Curlews, for example. A few species such as the woodpeckers and snipe produce sounds mechanically as well as vocally.

TERRITORY. Different bird species vary a great deal as regards the amount of territory needed by each pair. Some live and breed in colonies, like Rooks or Gannets, and are content with a 'territory' of only a few feet around each nest. Others like the Robin are highly territorial and fiercely defend their chosen patch. The spacing out of breeding pairs in this way has the effect of dividing up the available habitat and food more evenly, according to the needs of each species, so that each pair is better able to rear its young. It is remarkable how individual birds, when staking out their

territories each spring, tend to return to the places where they were raised. Swallows come back to the same barn, even after travelling many thousands of miles.

COURTSHIP. The first stage is usually the male's song, in some species combined with a special flight pattern, to lead the female to his territory or the nest-site he has chosen. When she arrives he follows this with a courtship display. These differ greatly from species to species but usually stress some feature of the plumage or posture. The Robin stretches up and puffs out his orange breast. Grebes shake their heads to show up their ruffs and 'ear-tufts'. The display may seem to consist of a number of apparently trivial items, but it all forms part of a complex inherited ritual, designed both to attract the female and to make sure that both birds become ready for breeding at the same time. Among birds that nest in colonies the display of one pair may be taken up by others, so that the whole colony prepares for breeding at the same time.

NESTS AND EGGS. Most birds build new nests each season, though large birds such as herons and eagles use old nests which they repair and redecorate. The parts played by the male and female in choosing a nest-site and in building the nest varies greatly from species to species. The nest itself may be as beautiful and elaborate as the Long-tailed Tit's mossy dome, or it may be just a bare ledge of rock, as with the Guillemot.

Once the nest is ready, the female starts to lay until the clutch is complete and she starts to brood. The clutch-size – the number of eggs laid – varies from the single egg of some seabirds to fifteen or so for a partridge, depending on various factors such as the number of young which the parents can feed and the number that may die before they become adults. Egg size and markings also differ widely. The markings are not always for concealment, though some, like terns' eggs, are marvellously camouflaged. Most hole-nesting birds, such as owls, lay white eggs. The eggs are incubated from 12 to around 40 days, according to species. Some chicks are hatched already downy, active and mobile, but most song-birds' chicks are helpless and have to stay in the nest until they fledge and can flutter away.

FOOD. Most birds are to some extent restricted in the food they eat, though Crows take almost anything. Smaller birds need proportionately more food than larger ones: a Blue Tit eats about a quarter of its own weight a day, while a Buzzard may average only 4%. Physical structure has much to do with the diet and how it is obtained: with their short legs and strong feet Blue Tits can forage along the thinnest twigs, while the heavier Great Tits feed more around the larger branches or trunk. The beaks of all birds are adapted to their kinds of food and methods of feeding.

MIGRATION. Most British birds can be classed either as summer or winter visitors, passage migrants or residents, but some species fall into more than one of these categories. Thus we see Chaffinches all year round, but in winter some of them will be continental birds who came in the autumn and will leave us in spring, while both in spring and autumn birds are passing through which breed further north and winter further south. Many of our waders are also passage migrants, some of them remaining to winter here in small numbers. The spring migration, when most birds are pressing on towards their breeding grounds, is a shorter and better defined movement than the gradual drift away in autumn. By July, some young Lapwings are already on their wintering grounds, although more northern bred birds may not reach them until November. In winter there is a good deal of movement in response to weather conditions, and flocking becomes a feature of birdlife.

WATCHING BIRDS. Many people are content just to be able to identify birds, and searching for rare birds, or species you have not seen before, is certainly exciting. On the other hand, there is still much to be learnt about the commoner birds with which this book deals, and observing them in your garden, a local park or around your home will give you a great deal of pleasure. In many ways it is best to concentrate on quite a small area which you can watch regularly and get to know well. Try to discover, for instance, how many pairs nest in it; how much space they seem to require; how successful they are in rearing their young; when do the cocks stop singing? In identifying birds there are plenty of problems when you come to the winter or immature plumages of even the common species, let alone rarities. Making notes is a good habit, too: it tends to sharpen the powers of observation, and can be useful and give you pleasure later. It is good to get to know other birdwatchers – perhaps by joining a local natural history or birdwatching society. And it is well worth joining the Royal Society for the Protection of Birds. The address to write to is The Lodge, Sandy, Bedfordshire.

Ducks, p. 22–25

GREAT CRESTED GREBE *(Podiceps cristatus)* 48cm. This is perhaps the most elegant of all the waterbirds. The beautiful ruff and crest appear on both sexes in spring, and the shining white foreneck can be seen clearly across the water at all seasons. It almost became extinct in Britain because of the demand for the satiny breast feathers, but it was protected and its numbers have increased dramatically since the last century. Courtship is spectacular. The ritual may vary in detail, but often the two birds approach each other with necks stretched low over the water, rise upright face-to-face, shaking their heads to display their spread ruffs, then present each other with scraps of waterweed. The nest is a floating pad of vegetation, often close by an old willow stump or amongst reeds, and the attractive, stripey chicks spend their early days on the adults' backs cradled between the raised wings. The Great Crested Grebe is widely distributed on the ponds, lakes and reservoirs of Britain, although it is less common in parts of the north and west. Many birds move to coastal waters in winter.

DABCHICK or LITTLE GREBE *(Tachybaptus ruficollis)* 27cm. The smallest of the swimming birds, recognizable by its blunt-tailed appearance. Like other grebes, it is always diving, disappearing abruptly and neatly when alarmed or merely fishing. It swims easily underwater with wide strokes of the large, lobed feet, and can stay submerged for up to half a minute. The nest is a mat of waterweed built up above the water level, and if an incubating bird is disturbed, it quickly covers the eggs with scraps of weed with a few flicks of the bill. It lives on ponds, dykes, flooded gravel pits, rivers and reservoirs throughout Britain, and is quite happy to occupy smaller and shallower areas of water than its larger cousin, as long as there is plenty of vegetation.

winter

GREAT CRESTED GREBE

summer

pullet

summer

winter

LITTLE GREBE

13

Common Gull
see p. 41

adult

imm.
1st
year

imm.
2nd year

GANNET

adult

FULMAR

14

GANNET *(Sula bassana)* 90cm. Nesting in about thirty colonies, some very large, around the coastal cliffs of north-west Europe, Gannets are a dramatic sight as they wheel about in their thousands over the surf. In autumn, though, the birds disperse widely across the Atlantic and North Sea. Although large, Gannets are lightly built, with a streamlined body and slender, powerful wings which may span six feet, and have a buoyant flight, alternately flapping and gliding. They plunge headlong into the water to catch fish, often from a height of fifty feet or more, and it is interesting that the nostrils do not open to the outside of the bill, so water cannot enter during a dive. Gannets lay a single egg, and the nest is a heap of seaweed and grass placed on a cliff-ledge or on the rocks or more sloping ground above.

FULMAR *(Fulmarus glacialis)* 47cm. This apparently gull-like bird is a member of the petrel and shearwater family, which have the nostrils set in a tube on the top of the bill, and has a characteristic stiff-winged sailing flight, the long glides alternating with brisk flapping. It nests on cliff ledges on many parts of Britain's coastline, and throughout the North Atlantic and Arctic oceans. It has increased dramatically in numbers in the last century, for reasons which are still unclear, but may, at any rate initially, have had much to do with the great increase in whaling and trawling and the consequent supply of fish-oil and refuse. The increase is still continuing, although at a slower rate, and potential new nest-sites are prospected each year.

MANX SHEARWATER *(Puffinus puffinus)* 35cm. Shearwaters are unmistakable as they flap and glide on stiff wings low over the water, canting and tilting so that the wing-tip almost furrows the waves. They nest in burrows or on grassy cliff-tops or islets along Britain's western seaboard from Scilly to St. Kilda, but in winter they desert British waters and may wander as far as the south Atlantic. They feed largely on fish, and the breeding colonies are very noisy at night, when the adult birds bring food back to their single fat, fluffy chick, who has had to wait all day for a meal.

Fulmar

**MANX
SHEARWATER**

SHAG *(Phalacrocorax aristotelis)* 76cm. The wave-washed rocks of our more rugged northern and western coasts are the typical haunt of the Shag. In Scotland it is far more abundant even than the Cormorant although, on the east and south-east coasts of England, there are breeding colonies at only one or two rocky sites. The Shag is often to be seen swimming happily in the churning surf below the cliffs, diving frequently for fish, and emerging now and then to perch on the rocks and stretch out its wings to dry. The waterproofing of its feathers, like those of the Cormorant, is less than in many other water birds.

CORMORANT *(Phalacrocorax carbo)* 91cm. A familiar bird around British coasts, flying low over the waves, with its neck stretched out and the wings beating strongly. Cormorants may also fly high up or even soar. It is more widely distributed than the Shag, although there are in fact fewer breeding pairs, and it more readily leaves the coast, visiting inland marshes, lakes and reservoirs, and sometimes perching on posts or trees. Indeed, at some sites it builds its bulky twig nest in bushes or trees. It is a voracious fisher, taking anything from conger-eels to sticklebacks, and swims easily, often with only the head and neck showing, and the bill pointed upwards. It often submerges with a little jump, catching its prey after an underwater chase.

SHAG

imm.

adult

adult
winter

CORMORANT

adult

imm.

adult
winter

17

imm.

adult

△
GREY HERON *(Ardea cinerea)* 91cm. Even at a distance the Heron is easily recognized in flight as it beats slowly across the sky on broad wings, its long neck drawn back between its shoulders. It is a skilled and patient fisherman, standing motionless but alert at the edge of a pond or stream as it waits for an unwary frog or fish to come within spearing distance. Eels are often caught on the marshes, and it is comic to watch the dismayed bird trying to deal with the slippery object squirming round its neck. Herons are widely distributed, and nest in colonies, building their large twig nests in tall trees or occasionally in reed beds. As a family, the herons are unusual in having patches of powder-down, which can be rubbed over the plumage with the beak to remove fish-slime and perhaps to help in waterproofing.

WHITE STORK *(Ciconia ciconia)* 102cm. Nowadays the Stork is only a rare visitor to Britain, but it is still traditionally known as a bringer of babies, and of good luck if it makes its bulky nest on your chimney. Unhappily, nesting storks are becoming a rare sight in western Europe, and only in the eastern and south-eastern areas, and in Spain and Portugal, is this handsome bird maintaining its numbers. Here it is not uncommon to see a pair stalking through the marshes or meadows on the lookout for frogs. It is a fine flier, and large flocks often soar to great heights while on their migration to or from Africa.

▽

imm.

adult

threat
posture

juv.

CANADA
GOOSE

MUTE
SWAN

GREYLAG GOOSE

20

Canada Goose

Greylag Goose

Mute swan

MUTE SWAN *(Cygnus olor)* 150cm. A royal bird in Britain since ancient times. Once truly wild in parts of eastern England, it was brought into semi-domestication by extensive trapping and pinioning in the Middle Ages, and highly valued both for adornment on moats or ponds, and for eating. It is a sociable bird, sometimes gathering in very large flocks, as at the famous and ancient swannery at Abbotsbury, in Dorset, although in the semi-artificial conditions in which it often lives it becomes aggressive towards other birds, threatening in the well-known posture with wings arched over the back. In flight swans are unmistakable, with their long necks stretched out and wings beating noisily. The Mute Swan is found throughout north-west Europe and has been increasing in numbers in recent years.

CANADA GOOSE *(Branta canadensis)* 100cm. As its name implies, this is a North American and Canadian bird. It was introduced to Europe more than 200 years ago and has become familiar on ornamental waters in England. It is also successfully naturalized in the south of Sweden. It seems to have become commoner in recent years, although it is still absent from some areas of Ireland and Scotland. It breeds mainly on lakes or meres, or in waterfowl collections, and in winter gathers into flocks which wander to coastal areas, marshes or river valleys, although small parties of non-breeding birds may be seen at any time, flying in V-shaped formation with characteristic honking calls.

GREYLAG GOOSE *(Anser anser)* 82cm. This fine bird now only breeds in the wild state in the extreme north of Scotland, the Hebrides, and in northern and eastern Europe. In winter, you may be lucky enough to find a flock of wild Greylags on some remote coastal marsh or estuary, but like all geese, they are wary and difficult to approach. Feral flocks, though, can be seen throughout the year in some parts of the country, notably the Norfolk broads, and Greylags are often kept in waterfowl collections.

△
SHELDUCK *(Tadorna tadorna)* 60cm. This handsomely marked duck, looking rather like a goose in build and flight, is common around the estuaries and coasts of Britain, especially where they are flat or sandy. Unusually for a duck, it nests in burrows or rabbit holes in sand dunes, or in bushy, hillocky areas wherever there is water nearby. The chicks are led to the water by their parents soon after hatching. In some parts of southern and eastern England, Shelduck can be found nesting far inland. It is a very gregarious bird, and the chicks from nearby nests pack together at an early age, often with only one set of parents to guard them. In the late summer, many migrate to the sandbanks off the coast of north-west Germany to undergo their annual moult, when they become flightless.

TEAL *(Anas crecca)* 35cm. The smallest of our ducks, the Teal has ◁ a particularly rapid flight; when disturbed, it rises off the water like a miniature rocket. It is a common bird in Britain, living on lakes and reservoirs, or at the coast in winter, and often nests by small heathy pools, or even away from water. In winter the resident population is swollen by immigrants from the far north and Russia.

MALLARD

juv. ♂

♂ eclipse

MALLARD *(Anas platyrhynchos)* 58cm. An adaptable and successful bird, the Mallard is by far the most familiar and widespread of our wild ducks, as well as being the ancestor of all our farmyard ducks. It breeds throughout Britain, and in many places its numbers are increased by artificial rearing and re-stocking. The nest is carefully hidden in grass, reeds or in undergrowth under hedges or even in woods, and up to 14 eggs are laid. The mother guards the chicks carefully and keeps them close to her on the move. After the breeding season the drakes moult their flight feathers and take on a protective "eclipse" plumage which makes them resemble the ducks. The fine glossy feathers of their winter and spring dress are not fully grown until September. Only the duck makes the typical farmyard quack; the drake has a grating, higher-pitched call.

SHOVELER *(Anas clypeata)* 51cm. With its breast sunk low in the water and its heavy bill held down, the Shoveler is an unmistakable sight on the lush fens and marshes of Britain. Although it is clumsy on land, and is a weaker flier than the Mallard, the Shoveler is the best adapted of all the surface-feeding ducks for dabbling. It sieves the water with its large, shovel-shaped bill for small animals or plants and rarely "up-ends".

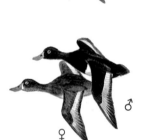

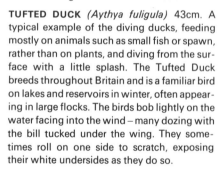

PINTAIL *(Anas acuta)* 56cm. Elegant and slender, Pintails sit high on the water with their long tails held up at an angle. They are one of the fastest ducks in flight. They breed in Scotland and south-east England, but are widely distributed in winter on lakes, estuaries and marshes. A very wary bird; you will have to approach a flock carefully if you want to watch them dabbling on the mud at low tide.

TUFTED DUCK *(Aythya fuligula)* 43cm. A typical example of the diving ducks, feeding mostly on animals such as small fish or spawn, rather than on plants, and diving from the surface with a little splash. The Tufted Duck breeds throughout Britain and is a familiar bird on lakes and reservoirs in winter, often appearing in large flocks. The birds bob lightly on the water facing into the wind – many dozing with the bill tucked under the wing. They sometimes roll on one side to scratch, exposing their white undersides as they do so.

POCHARD *(Aythya ferina)* 46cm. Freshwater lakes or ponds and reservoirs are the typical habitat of the Pochard. It is rather shy, swimming well away from the shore, and when nervous can sink so that the wavelets wash across its back. It is difficult to count the number of birds in a flock because they keep diving and bobbing up in different places. It is widespread in winter but is a rather uncommon breeding bird in Britain.

SHOVELER

♀

♂

juv.

PINTAIL

♀

♂

TUFTED DUCK

POCHARD

♀

♂

25

GOLDEN EAGLE

GOLDEN EAGLE *(Aquila chrysaetos)* 85cm. Having survived the relentless shooting and trapping of the last century by retreating to the wild and lonely mountainous areas of Scotland's highlands and islands, this magnificent bird has suffered more recently from the poisonous chemicals used in sheep-dips. Fortunately some 250 pairs remain, but to most of Britain it is only an extremely rare visitor. Usually first seen gliding above some heather-covered hillside, every now and then giving a powerful, heavy flap of its wings, it also soars majestically with the primary feathers splayed out like spread fingers. When it sights a grouse or mountain hare it falls in a long dive to overhaul its prey, killing solely by the extremely powerful grasp of the heavy feet and claws. It readily feeds on carrion, and has been known to take birds as large as a Greylag Goose. It has a thrilling display flight, in which both birds "power-dive" at each other at great heights. The huge stick nest, placed in a tall pine or on a cliff-face, is used and added to year after year.

BUZZARD

BUZZARD *(Buteo buteo)* 55cm. The commonest large hawk of Britain and Europe, it is usually seen soaring over hills or woods on its broad rounded wings, and has a plaintive squealing note which can be heard while the bird is still high in the air. It usually appears singly or in pairs but sometimes gathers in quite large flocks, the circling, floating figures spiralling higher and higher in a favourable up-draught. It is commonest as a breeding bird in Scotland, Wales and north and west England, but also nests regularly in some areas of south and south-east England. The large stick nest is built in a tree or amongst the heather on a steep hillside, and two or three eggs are laid. Buzzards feed largely on small mammals and insects, and catch their prey by dropping on it rather than chasing it. The plumage is very variable, the most normal variety being dark brown above and paler below.

Colour phases in Buzzard

27

♀

imm.

♂

SPARROWHAWK *(Accipiter nisus)* 34cm. The ravages of gamekeepers and, in the last twenty years, of pesticides, have reduced what was once a common hawk to extinction in parts of eastern and southern Britain. However, it still lives in fair numbers as a woodland resident elsewhere. Although taking pheasant chicks on occasion, Sparrowhawks feed largely on songbirds, which are caught in flight, usually after a dashing chase, or taken by surprise as the hawk sweeps over a hedge into a feeding flock. Often, the only evidence that a hawk is around is a tell-tale heap of feathers, although you may catch a glimpse of it flying rapidly across a glade or ride. The bulky twig nest is usually built in a tall tree deep in the woods, and four or five eggs are laid.

KESTREL *(Falco tinnunculus)* 34cm. By far the commonest bird of prey in Britain and Europe, the Kestrel is well-known through its characteristic method of searching for prey. It hangs in the air, wings flickering and tail spread, as it scans the ground below for a mouse or grasshopper; if disappointed at first, it may side-slip a few feet and continue hovering, or fly off to try elsewhere. When prey is sighted, the hovering height is often lowered in several stages, until the final vertical stoop with closed wings. The Kestrel has shorter and stouter legs than the bird-catching hawks. Common in open or lightly wooded country, it can often make a good living nowadays from the wide motorway verges. In woodland it may appropriate an old crow's nest, but often lays the eggs directly onto a ledge of a cliff or tall building.

Pheasant

♂

♀

Redlegged
Partridge

♀

♂

PARTRIDGE

♀

PHEASANT

30

PARTRIDGE *(Perdix perdix)* 30cm. Walking across a stubble field or pasture, you may well be startled by a Partridge as it rises explosively from the ground and whirrs away on rounded, down-curved wings, alternately flapping and gliding, then skimming over a hedge and alighting in the next field. The rufous tail feathers are conspicuously fanned as the bird comes in to land, often running on a little as if unable to stop properly. Although still common, Partridges are decreasing in numbers. The **Red-legged Partridge** *(Alectoris rufa)*, an introduced species, is a little larger and paler, lacking the dark horseshoe belly mark. It often prefers drier pastures, and is found widely throughout Britain.

'Ringneck'   'Old English'   melanistic

PHEASANT *(Phasianus colchicus)* 76cm (male) 53cm (female). This very familiar gamebird was probably brought to Britain from the Caucasus by the Romans. In the wild state it is found from south-east Russia to Burma and China, where the birds normally have the familiar white collar. The variation in the plumage of cock Pheasants in Britain is the result of importing different races of pheasant at different times. Although it is a hardy bird, quite capable of surviving unprotected, game preservation undoubtedly helps to maintain a large Pheasant population, and there has probably been some increase even in the last few years. Pheasants are shy birds, and if possible will run for cover rather than fly, with the neck lowered and outstretched. The cock's resonant crowing is a familiar woodland sound in spring.

♂
'Ringneck'

△
MOORHEN *(Gallinula chloropus)* 33cm. Hardly any pond, ornamental lake or soggy ditch throughout Britain is without its pair of Moorhens. It is a pugnacious bird, though, and defends its territory fiercely, so a small pond will only hold a single pair. A successful and adaptable species, it is as happy on land as in the water, where it is a good though rather jerky swimmer, its head bobbing as it paddles along. Although often grazing in fields or parks well away from cover, Moorhens are wary, always ready to run back to the waterside vegetation, with heads down and tails flirted to show the patches of white. They feed on grain and seeds as well as water plants, and tread delicately over the floating vegetation on their long toes. The nest – a pad of rushes and grass – is built by the water's edge, or more conspicuously anchored among the growing reeds out in the pond.

COOT *(Fulica atra)* 38cm. More thoroughly aquatic than the Moorhen, the Coot has large lobes along the sides of its toes, which help it to paddle. It swims smoothly, preferring more open stretches of water, and often gathers in large flocks in winter on lakes and reservoirs. Quite a strong flier when once up, it has some trouble in taking off, and has to patter along the surface before getting airborne. It is even more quarrelsome and aggressive than the Moorhen and fights are frequent, although they rarely end in injury. Feeding on aquatic animals and plants, Coots are regular divers, and although they sometimes feed on grassy banks by the water, they are much less dependent on land for food than are Moorhens.

MOORHEN ♂ ♀

COOT ♂ ♀

33

△
LAPWING *(Vanellus vanellus)* 30cm. Lapwing flocks are a familiar sight in the countryside in winter, flickering black and white as the birds flap unsteadily along on their broad wings, their tracks crossing and crisscrossing as they swoop in to land. In early spring they disperse to water-meadows and rough pastures where the cock performs his tumbling display flight, calling his shrill, wheezy "kie-vit". Both birds defend their territory aggressively, and any marauding crow or magpie is harried unmercifully. The nest is often very difficult to find, and is a sparsely lined hollow on the ground or in a clump of grass. They lay four speckled eggs. Lapwings breed throughout Britain, and the non-breeding and young birds are back in small flocks, prospecting their winter quarters, by the end of June. Some flocks, however, migrate long distances, and may spend the winter as far away as North Africa. Occasionally some even cross the Atlantic and are found in North America.

LITTLE RINGED PLOVER *(Charadrius dubius)* 15cm. You should be able to tell this bird from the commoner Ringed Plover by its all-dark wing, and short, low call. It breeds in more southerly areas and migrates annually to its winter home by the Mediterranean or in Africa. It nests on sandy or stony ground by fresh water, in England often in sand or gravel pits, where it seems oblivious to the noisy earth-moving machinery.

RINGED PLOVER *(Charadrius hiaticula)* 19cm. This lively and attractive plover is soon noticed on sandy or shingly beaches. It runs about continuously, its legs twinkling over the sand, stopping now and again to bob down and pick up a sandhopper, or flies out over the water, showing its white wing-bar. The call-note, often heard, is a pretty double whistle "too-lee". The fussy parents will try to lure intruders away from the vicinity of the chicks – little speckly balls of fluff which can run surprisingly fast.

KENTISH PLOVER *(Charadrius alexandrinus)* 15cm. More a bird of sandy coasts than its two close relatives, it is now only a visitor to Britain. Beware of confusing it with the young of the other species, which also have incomplete breast bands, but pale, not dark, legs.

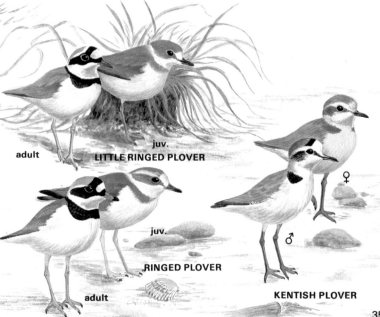

adult   juv.
LITTLE RINGED PLOVER

juv.
RINGED PLOVER

adult

♀

♂

KENTISH PLOVER

△
CURLEW *(Numenius arquata)* 55cm. A wary bird of mudflats, estuaries or rocky coasts in winter, the Curlew nests commonly on moors and hill pastures in north and eastern Britain, and widely though more locally through much of England except in the south-east. It makes a beautiful liquid, rippling call during the display flight over the breeding grounds, but the loud, wild note from which it gets its name is as familiar on the shore as it is in the hills. Although sometimes seen singly or in small parties, Curlews often gather in huge flocks in the winter, like the smaller waders, and although they do not indulge in the same aerial manoeuvres, they have a fast, direct flight.

DUNLIN *(Calidris alpina)* 18cm. This is usually the commonest of the small shorebirds in winter, and often occurs in dense flocks which twist and turn in flight with great precision, all the undersides flashing white together as the birds simultaneously change direction. Dunlins breed on highland moors and in rough grazing pastures in the hills in Scotland and northern England, and in parts of Ireland and Wales. The male has a rather lark-like display flight over the breeding territory, rising and falling high against the sky as he utters his trilling song. The young birds in autumn are often very tame and can be approached closely as they feed along the tideline in twos and threes; like the adults when in winter plumage, they lack the black belly patch. The timing of plumage changes in the Dunlin is very erratic, though, and sometimes adult birds in winter plumage can still be seen in mid-summer.

REDSHANK

REDSHANK *(Tringa totanus)* 28cm. Shy and noisy, the Redshank has been aptly called the "warden of the marshes". Both on its breeding ground in the lush water-meadows, and on the cold saltings in winter, it flies up with a loud triple whistle, showing the white patches on the back and at the rear of the wings, and quickly spreads the alarm to other shorebirds. The nest is hidden in a thick tussock in a marsh or swampy field, and the parent bird keeps an eye on any intruder from a vantage point on a fence or post, scolding and bobbing nervously on its long legs. In his display flight, the male rises with fluttering wings as he whistles, and sinks slowly to earth, still singing, to stand for a moment with wings raised as he alights. Most of our Redshanks are resident, moving to the coast in winter.

winter

summer

DUNLIN

37

winter

OYSTERCATCHER

summer

SNIPE

WOODCOCK

38

OYSTERCATCHER *(Haematopus ostralegus)* 43cm. Perhaps the most striking of the shorebirds, with its pied plumage and long, red bill. It has a loud musical whistle "kleeep", often called by birds in flight, or especially in the communal display, when a party of birds walks about crying excitedly, with heads lowered and bills pointing down. It is very common on all coasts, and the winter flocks on sandy estuaries or mud-flats may number thousands of individuals. Although it has increased greatly in the last seventy years, it is becoming more and more subject to disturbance from holiday-makers, as it nests near the shore on shingle or rough grass.

SNIPE *(Gallinago gallinago)* 27cm. Usually the best view to be had of a Snipe is when the slim brownish bird with long bill rockets up from a ditch or boggy patch, twisting and turning in flight, and making its harsh call-note. A more leisurely view of one probing the mud at the edge of a marsh reveals the beautifully striped and mottled plumage. Snipe make a curious soft drumming sound in their undulating display flight, caused by vibration of their stiff outer tail feathers in the air as they dive.

WOODCOCK *(Scolopax rusticola)* 34cm. As its name implies, this is a bird of woodland, despite its family relationship with the shorebirds, and spends the day roosting in dead leaves under a bramble or rhododendron thicket. At dusk it flies to nearby streams or boggy ground to probe for worms with the aid of its very sensitive and flexible bill-tip. After much argument, it has been established that a Woodcock can carry her young away from a threatened nest, holding them between the thighs. In autumn, many cross the North Sea and land on the east coast dunes before dispersing inland.

imm.

adult
winter

adult

COMMON
GULL

adult

HERRING GULL

LESSER
BLACK-BACK

GREATER
BLACK-BACK

40

COMMON GULL *(Larus canus)* 40cm. It is quite easy to distinguish between the familiar "sea-gulls", although many people do not take the trouble to do so. The Common Gull breeds in colonies in Scotland and N. Ireland. In winter it seldom strays far out to sea, although it is common inland. It joins other gulls around harbours and beaches, hovering above the breakers as it keeps a sharp look-out for anything edible.

HERRING GULL *(Larus argentatus)* 56cm. The commonest gull of coastal areas, breeding both on rocky islets or cliffs, and on coastal constructions or on buildings in towns. Powerful and aggressive, it steals eggs and chicks from seabird colonies, or carries crabs or molluscs into the air to drop them on rocks below, swooping down to pick out the contents. Graceful and effortless in flight, it can soar to great heights, appearing as no more than a white speck in the sky.

LESSER BLACK-BACK *(Larus fuscus)* 54cm. You will often see these gulls following cross-channel boats, floating lightly in the wind, side-slipping and shifting places in the flock as they scan the wake for food. They are less restricted to the coast for breeding than Herring Gulls, and more often migrate south for the winter. They nest on sand dunes, moors or rocky islands, often in large colonies. Wintering flocks in Britain have grown much larger in the last twenty years.

GREATER BLACK-BACK *(Larus marinus)* 74cm. A rapacious and vicious pirate among seabirds, this large gull is often seen far out to sea. Although not numerous, it is a regular and conspicuous visitor to coasts and harbours in winter, feeding on offal, fish or animals, and causing havoc in seabird colonies. A small flock has even been seen harrying a Dunlin in flight, one of the gulls eventually catching and swallowing it.

adult

adult

imm.

adult

adult

**adult
summer**

BLACK-HEADED GULL *(Larus ridibundus)* 38cm. This is the commonest small gull in Britain, with a confusing sequence of plumages which vary according to both age and season. It is a noisy, sociable bird, often nesting in large colonies, and is just as common inland as it is by the coast – in fact, it is seldom seen far out to sea. It has increased greatly in numbers in the last seventy years, following a major decline last century, and is also becoming commoner over western Europe as a whole. It is light and buoyant, almost tern-like, in flight, and is agile enough to catch flying insects on the wing. You will often see a flapping, jostling crowd following the plough to pick up worms and grubs as they are uncovered. It also feeds on a wide variety of other vegetable and animal matter, and, like other gulls, sometimes patters on the wet mud to bring worms to the surface. Most birds are year-round residents of Britain, although some travel as far south as Spain for the winter.

adult
winter

1st year winter

juv.

1st year
winter

adult
moulting

adult
winter

43

COMMON TERN *(Sterna hirundo)* 35cm. A common summer visitor to the coasts of Britain. Terns are often called "Sea Swallows" because of their graceful, easy flight and forked tails; the pointed wings beat flexibly and deeply as the bird flies into the wind over the breakers, its head bent down as it watches for fish. A momentary flicker as it hovers is followed by the characteristic headlong plunge, and before the splash has subsided the bird emerges, with a glistening fish in its bill. Sometimes the dive is fruitless, and the bird may check its descent, or alight momentarily on the water with wings raised. They nest in noisy colonies on sand dunes, shingle or low islets around the coast, and the birds defend their nest-sites fiercely.

LITTLE TERN *(Sterna albifrons)* 20cm. Nesting on shingle or sandy beaches, the attractive Little Tern has become much rarer around Britain's coastline in the last thirty years, and the influx of holidaymakers must be at least partly to blame. Smaller than the other sea terns, it flies with quicker wing-beats, and is much less sociable. Colonies seldom reach 100 pairs, and often only a pair or two share a stretch of beach. It is a noisy bird, with a scolding "kik kik kik" flight note.

COMMON TERN   **LITTLE TERN**

BLACK TERN *(Chlidonias niger)* 24cm. A bird of fresh rather than salt ▷ water, breeding on marshes or flooded fields, although on migration it can often be seen in large flocks over the sea. It does not plunge for fish, but dips daintily to the surface to catch aquatic insects, and has a rather wavering, erratic flight. The Black Tern stopped breeding regularly in Britain a century ago, but it has nested occasionally in the last few years, and might become established again given the right conditions. It is a common bird of passage, and often looks very patchy in autumn when moulting to winter plumage.

COMMON TERN
winter

adult

juv.

LITTLE
TERN

moulting

juv.

BLACK
TERN

breeding

winter

45

breeding colony

PUFFIN *(Fratercula arctica)* 30cm. A distinctive and colourful summer visitor, mainly to northern and western coasts. Like the other members of the auk family shown here, Puffins spend the winter at sea, and return to their breeding sites in early spring. They nest in burrows on grassy slopes on cliff-tops, and some of the colonies are huge, although numbers have declined severely in recent years. Puffins are good swimmers and divers, and expert at stacking fish crossways in the bill when feeding the chick, sometimes bringing back up to eleven at once.

RAZORBILL *(Alca torda)* 40cm. Nesting in the more sheltered corners and crannies in cliffs, or amongst boulders and rock debris, Razorbills are more evenly distributed around our northern and western coasts than Puffins, although they are actually much less numerous. They winter far out to sea and return to their nest-sites early in the New Year, a week or two after the Guillemots. They lay a single, oval egg which is less pointed and so less roll-proof than that of the Guillemot.

GUILLEMOT *(Uria aalge)* 42cm. The most numerous of our seabirds, and the most commonly seen around the coast in winter. It is often a bedraggled victim of oil-spills. Breeding colonies are widely distributed, avoiding only the flatter stretches of our eastern and southern coasts. Some colonies in Scotland may hold up to 70,000 pairs. Guillemots spend much time on the water, diving for fish and catching them after a brief chase. They have a rapid whirring flight on their narrow wings, often following each other in long lines low over the water. The birds make no nests and the single, rather large egg is sharply pointed at one end; its shape prevents it from rolling off the narrow cliff ledges on which it is laid. Often the birds sit so close together that the eggs are laid side-by-side. The "bridled" form is a variety which as a breeding bird becomes progressively commoner northwards.

imm.

adult

PUFFIN

Razorbills

Puffin in winter

RAZORBILL

adult

imm.

adult

in winter

"bridled"

northern

southern

both in winter

GUILLEMOT

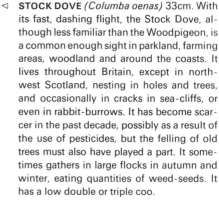

◁ **STOCK DOVE** *(Columba oenas)* 33cm. With its fast, dashing flight, the Stock Dove, although less familiar than the Woodpigeon, is a common enough sight in parkland, farming areas, woodland and around the coasts. It lives throughout Britain, except in north-west Scotland, nesting in holes and trees, and occasionally in cracks in sea-cliffs, or even in rabbit-burrows. It has become scarcer in the past decade, possibly as a result of the use of pesticides, but the felling of old trees must also have played a part. It sometimes gathers in large flocks in autumn and winter, eating quantities of weed-seeds. It has a low double or triple coo.

◁ **WOODPIGEON** *(Columba palumbus)* 40cm. A familiar, heavily-built and handsome bird. Understandably shy in country districts, where it is shot as a pest, the woodpigeon can be watched at close quarters in town parks, where it is often to be seen consorting with feral pigeons. Most British Wood-pigeons seem to be year-round residents, although large numbers migrate southward in Europe in late autumn, and many of them cross the North Sea to swell the flocks of our own birds. They do much damage to cereal and vegetable crops although, among other things, they also eat weed-seeds. The nest is a flimsy twig platform in a tall hedge or tree, and two round white eggs are laid. The young "squabs" feed at first on a curd-like secretion from the adult's crop, called "pigeon's milk".

◁ **FERAL DOVE** *(Columba livia)* 33cm. The common town pigeon, descended from lost or strayed domestic pigeons which were themselves descended from wild Rock Doves. The domestic variety is recorded from the Middle East as long as 5,000 years ago. They generally resemble the wild dove, although there are many different plumage types – the "blue chequer" is common among racing pigeons.

STOCK DOVE

juv.

adult

WOOD PIGEON

juv.

adult

FERAL DOVE

49

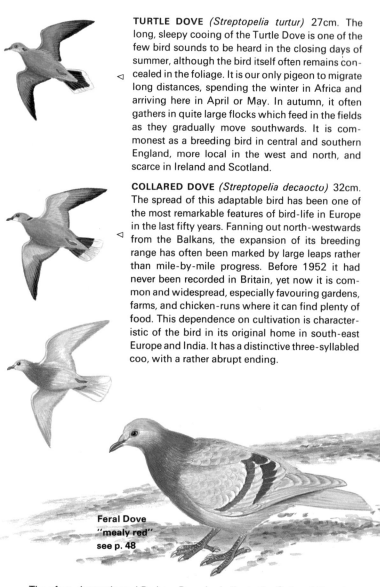

TURTLE DOVE *(Streptopelia turtur)* 27cm. The long, sleepy cooing of the Turtle Dove is one of the few bird sounds to be heard in the closing days of summer, although the bird itself often remains concealed in the foliage. It is our only pigeon to migrate long distances, spending the winter in Africa and arriving here in April or May. In autumn, it often gathers in quite large flocks which feed in the fields as they gradually move southwards. It is commonest as a breeding bird in central and southern England, more local in the west and north, and scarce in Ireland and Scotland.

COLLARED DOVE *(Streptopelia decaocto)* 32cm. The spread of this adaptable bird has been one of the most remarkable features of bird-life in Europe in the last fifty years. Fanning out north-westwards from the Balkans, the expansion of its breeding range has often been marked by large leaps rather than mile-by-mile progress. Before 1952 it had never been recorded in Britain, yet now it is common and widespread, especially favouring gardens, farms, and chicken-runs where it can find plenty of food. This dependence on cultivation is characteristic of the bird in its original home in south-east Europe and India. It has a distinctive three-syllabled coo, with a rather abrupt ending.

Feral Dove "mealy red" see p. 48

The often-domesticated Barbary Dove is similar to the Collared Dove but paler, and lacks the black primaries; beware of confusion with the brown and grey forms of the "London" or semi-domesticated pigeons.

TURTLE DOVE

imm.

adult

juv.

COLLARED DOVE

adult

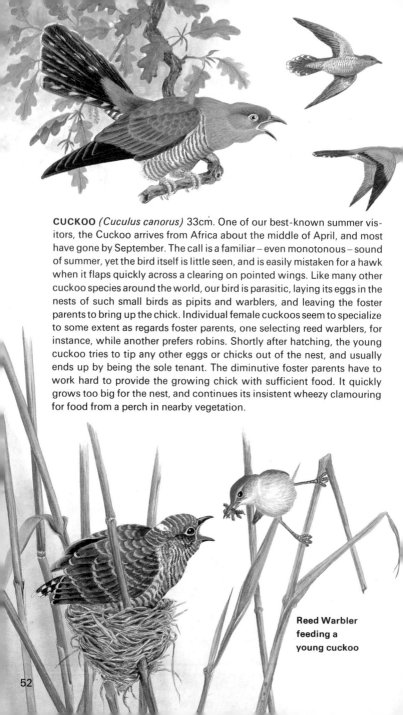

CUCKOO *(Cuculus canorus)* 33cm. One of our best-known summer visitors, the Cuckoo arrives from Africa about the middle of April, and most have gone by September. The call is a familiar – even monotonous – sound of summer, yet the bird itself is little seen, and is easily mistaken for a hawk when it flaps quickly across a clearing on pointed wings. Like many other cuckoo species around the world, our bird is parasitic, laying its eggs in the nests of such small birds as pipits and warblers, and leaving the foster parents to bring up the chick. Individual female cuckoos seem to specialize to some extent as regards foster parents, one selecting reed warblers, for instance, while another prefers robins. Shortly after hatching, the young cuckoo tries to tip any other eggs or chicks out of the nest, and usually ends up by being the sole tenant. The diminutive foster parents have to work hard to provide the growing chick with sufficient food. It quickly grows too big for the nest, and continues its insistent wheezy clamouring for food from a perch in nearby vegetation.

**Reed Warbler
feeding a
young cuckoo**

HOOPOE *(Upupa epops)* 28cm. A regular but rather scarce visitor to Britain, the Hoopoe is a striking bird of woodlands or orchards. It nests in tree-holes, and has bred from time to time in this country, but owing to its tameness and gaudy appearance it was often shot; if left alone it might have been encouraged to nest more often. It is usually seen pecking about on lawns or paths, raising the crest when alarmed or as it alights in a tree. It has a slow, rather wavering flight on its broad, barred wings. The low, mellow note from which it gets its name carries a surprising distance. It is a summer visitor to Europe, wintering in Africa.

KINGFISHER *(Alcedo atthis)* 17cm. All too often, the Kingfisher is only seen as a flash of electric blue as it speeds off over a pool or along a stream. You will be lucky ◁ to come across one without startling it, as it watches for fish from a post or a willow twig, the heavy bill pointing downwards. A sudden drop into the water, and then it is back on its perch with a minnow or stickleback which it stuns with a blow or two on the branch, and then swallows head-first. The nest, in a tunnel in a river-bank, is a smelly, messy affair, littered with fish-bones. A widespread bird in Britain, rarer in Scotland, its numbers are much affected by bad winters and river pollution.

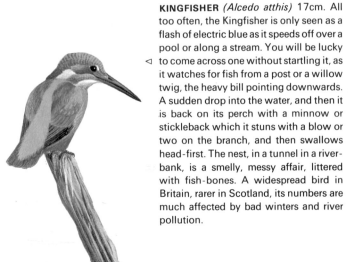

BARN OWL *(Tyto alba)* 34cm. The sight of a ghostly white owl, as it hunts in the gathering dusk, with erratic and wavering flight along a hedge, is unhappily becoming an unusual event in many areas. As available nesting sites in old barns or big trees with suitable holes become fewer, so this attractive bird diminishes in numbers, although it will quite readily take to artificial nest-boxes to roost or nest in. Barn Owls should be given every protection, for they are very beneficial in keeping down the number of rats and mice. They have a variety of calls, the most common being a loud shriek. They also make hissing and snoring noises, especially the young birds, who are very entertaining to watch, with their knock-kneed stance and swaying, stretching, threat postures.

TAWNY OWL *(Strix aluco)* 38cm. The well-known long, wavering hoot of this owl is nowadays as much a feature of suburban gardens and town parks as it is of country woods. The Tawny Owl is, nevertheless, essentially a woodland bird, and is rarely seen in daylight, but when a drowsy bird is discovered roosting against a tree-trunk by some foraging tit or creeper it has no peace. A noisy crowd of small birds quickly gathers to mob the common enemy until it flaps off in disgust. Owls usually nest in a hollow tree, where three or four large white eggs are laid. They are fierce protectors of their possessions, and have been known to attack intruders on many occasions. It is absent from Ireland, where its place is taken by the Long-eared Owl.

LONG-EARED OWL *(Asio otus)* 36cm. The most nocturnal of our owls. It is rather more partial to fir-woods and plantations than the Tawny Owl, and in most parts of the country it is less common than it used to be, possibly as a result of competition with the Tawny. It is probably much overlooked, although the low, rather mournful hoot is a good guide to its presence in the breeding season. In winter it becomes more sociable, and roosts in groups of up to twenty in thick hawthorn scrub. It often nests in an old crow's nest, although it may occasionally build on the ground at the foot of a tree. The eggs are laid early, often in March.

LITTLE OWL *(Athene noctua)* 22cm. Following its introduction to this country from the Continent some ninety years ago, this is now our most familiar owl in farmland, parks and light woodland. It is often active in daytime, especially in the winter, and is noisy in the late afternoons in early spring, the loud, rather cat-like call carrying far over the fields from its favourite perch in an old willow. When it becomes aware that it is being watched, the Little Owl ducks and bobs comically as it glares at the intruder with yellow eyes, and on too close an approach if flaps off with typically bounding flight, often swooping down from the branch as it takes off. It nests in hollow trees, being especially fond of pollarded willows. It is absent from Ireland, and only a rare breeder in Scotland.

55

adult
♂

juv.

♀

bounding flight

△
GREAT SPOTTED WOODPECKER *(Dendrocopus major)* 23cm. The characteristic loud drumming sound made by this handsome wood-pecker is a courtship call, produced by tapping or vibrating the bill rapidly against a dead bough. The bird has favourite drumming boughs, no doubt hollow ones which are the most resonant, and also has a loud, abrupt alarm-call. Woodpeckers are shy birds but can, with care, be watched as they work their way up a tree, tapping here and there, but as soon as they become aware of being watched, they slip round to the other side of the trunk, or fly off with a bounding action to a safer distance. The nest hole is usually hacked out of rotten wood, often at a considerable height, and the six or so eggs are laid at the bottom of a shaft up to a foot deep.

GREEN WOODPECKER *(Picus viridis)* 32cm. Probably the best known of our woodpeckers. Because of its passion for ants, it is quite often seen on the ground, especially on lawns, where it makes large holes with its powerful bill. The noisy laughing cry is heard continuously in the spring and, although it does not drum regularly like the Great Spotted Woodpecker, it certainly taps the wood as it searches along the branches for insects and grubs in the bark. When flying, which it does with an easy bounding action, the yellow rump is conspicuous and the bird is sometimes optimistically mistaken for a Golden Oriole. When courting, several birds join together to chase in spirals up the trunk of a tree, calling excitedly. Both birds join in boring out the nest hole, which is larger than those of other woodpeckers, and not infrequently a nesting pair are dispossessed by Starlings, which find the hole just the right size. It is a bird of open country with scattered trees, and parkland rather than thick woods, and although absent from Ireland, both this species and the Great Spotted Woodpecker are common residents elsewhere in Britain, the Green being more local in Scotland.

▽

juv.

♀

♂

SWIFT

HOUSE MARTIN

juv.

SWALLOWS

SWIFT *(Apus apus)* 16cm. The parties of screaming Swifts which dash between buildings ▷ or low over the meadows are a feature of summer evenings; later the birds circle so high as to become invisible in the gathering dusk. Some may even spend the night on the wing, although paired birds seem to return to the nest-site, on rafters or in crevice in masonry, to roost. The height at which Swifts fly depends on the level of insect flight, and this is partly governed by the weather, thundery conditions often causing higher flying. Swifts are late immigrants, arriving at the end of April, and quickly set about nesting. Once the young have left the nest they are ready to migrate, leaving before their parents.

HOUSE MARTIN *(Delichon urbica)* 12cm. ▷ Sometimes confused with Swallows, House Martins are easily distinguished by their white rumps, best seen as the birds swoop up to their rounded mud nests under the eaves. They are sociable birds, and many nests can be seen stuck along the wall of a favourite building, side by side, tucked under a ledge or tiles. The birds hang by the nest twittering, then spread their wings to drop away, circle round and up again. When gathering to migrate, they line up on wires like Swallows.

SWALLOW *(Hirundo rustica)* 19cm. Perhaps ▷ our best-loved summer visitor, the Swallow breeds over a huge area, ranging from America and Europe to China, before migrating to the tropics for the winter. In spring the Swallows return to nest in our sheds and outhouses, each individual making for the district in which it was reared, and often to the same farm or shed. The nest is always supported from below, by a beam or joist, unlike that of the Martin. The twittering song, often uttered as the bird perches on a wire or in a courtship chase, is particularly sweet and attractive.

Δ

CRESTED LARK *(Galerida cristata)* 17cm. A common roadside bird of continental Europe, which, rather surprisingly, has only been identified some fifteen times in Britain. Although it has a very wide breeding range, from Europe and North Africa to India, it is a sedentary bird, much less given to travelling than the Skylark. It is fond of basking and dust-bathing on sandy paths and bare places. When it flies up, the rather rounded wings and buff, as opposed to white, outer tail feathers clearly distinguish it from our more familiar bird. It does not compare as a songster with the Skylark, nor does it rise so high in the air when singing; often it remains sitting on a low perch.

SKYLARK *(Alauda arvensis)* 18cm. One of the most characteristic bird sounds of open country and farmland is the Skylark's celebrated song – lively, sustained and chirruping. The bird mounts rather jerkily in the air, as if being pulled up on a thread, and circles with fluttering wings for several minutes before dropping silently to earth. On occasion the song is uttered from a perch on a post or wall. Although Skylarks are with us all the year, their numbers are swelled in autumn as birds from northern Europe pass through southwards, and again in spring during the return passage. Bad weather during the winter is often accompanied by emigration on a massive scale as the birds seek better conditions.

SKYLARK

MEADOW PIPIT *(Anthus pratensis)*
14cm. Abundant on moors, saltings, dunes and heathland throughout ▷ Britain, this is the little brown streaky bird that rises from the grass with a thin, repeated call and flies jerkily away, showing the white outer tail feathers. In winter the birds leave the higher and more desolate moors, and form small flocks in the lowlands and along the saltings, and in spring and autumn are joined by continental and Icelandic birds passing through. The cock has a simple twittering song, uttered during a short fluttering flight above the breeding ground; he takes off from the ground, and generally returns there rather than to a perch, descending parachute-like on stiffly-spread wings. The nest is well concealed in a clump of rushes, grass or heather, and is a favourite foster-home for cuckoos.

PIED
WAGTAIL

WHITE
WAGTAIL

GREY
WAGTAIL

YELLOW
WAGTAIL

BLUE-HEADED
WAGTAIL

PIED WAGTAIL *(Motacilla alba)* 18cm. There is no mistaking the slim form of the Pied Wagtail as it runs quickly over a lawn to snap at a fly, or catches insects among the feet of grazing cattle. Always on the move, it bobs the tail constantly; it takes a short bounding flight up to the roof of a cowshed, runs nimbly along, and flutters up to take the dancing midges. The thin double call-note "chizzick" is often uttered, although the twittering song is only infrequently heard. While not as fond of running water as the Grey Wagtail, it loves wet meadows, pool margins and puddles, especially in farmyards, and can often be seen running along the furrows of a ploughed field. It breeds widely in Britain, and most of our birds migrate to southern Europe for the winter. Birds of the Continental race, *M.a.alba*, the **White Wagtail**, which visit us on passage, are best told in spring when the cocks have a clear grey back.

imm.

winter
adult

GREY WAGTAIL *(Motacilla cinerea)* 18cm. The long tail gives an extra touch of elegance to this attractive wagtail. A bird or rivers and streams, especially in hilly districts, it is commonest as a breeding bird in northern and western Britain. It runs easily over the water-washed rocks or sits, tail wagging, on a branch over a stream to watch for passing flies. Mainly a resident species, it is commoner in the lowlands in winter, by lake or river-sides. At this season the cock, having lost the black chin patch of spring, resembles the hen.

imm.

adult
♀

YELLOW/BLUE-HEADED WAGTAIL *(Motacilla flava)* 17cm. When the cock Yellow Wagtails arrive in spring from their winter quarters in Africa, they are a brilliant, eye-catching gold, but they become much browner and duller in late summer. Breeding commonly in England in water-meadows, fields and marshes, the Yellow Wagtail is virtually absent from Ireland and Scotland. It is replaced by other races abroad, most breeding cocks in western Europe having blue-grey heads, but as a species is very variable, and shades from white to dark grey may sometimes be seen.

imm.

adult
♀

WHITETHROAT *(Sylvia communis)* 14cm. The scratchy little song, uttered as the bird dances about in the air over a patch of gorse or bushes, is a pleasing reminder that spring has arrived. Whitethroats winter in Africa, and nest in bushy places or scrub over most of Britain except in the far north. The population has not yet recovered from the sharp drop in the number of breeding pairs in 1969 caused by heavy mortality in the winter as a result of drought. When the cock is singing – which he often does from the topmost twig on a hedge – his throat is puffed out, drawing attention to its whiteness, and the crest feathers raised.

GARDEN WARBLER *(Sylvia borin)* 14cm. This is one of the most soberly coloured of the warblers, although the lack of distinctive markings enhances its full, dark eye. While not much to look at, it is renowned for its beautiful song, which is like the Blackcap's, only more sustained. It is a bird of thick undergrowth in scrub or woodland, and is often difficult to see. A late summer migrant, it is not here in any numbers until mid-May, and has the shortest song-period of our commoner warblers. It is widely distributed in England and Wales, but uncommon in Ireland and north-west Scotland.

DUNNOCK

DUNNOCK *(Prunella modularis)* 15cm. Inconspicuous yet by no means shy, the Hedge Sparrow, as it is sometimes called, can often be seen hopping about quietly amongst the fallen leaves by a hedge or path. It has a rather thin but pleasant little song, which is performed frequently from March onwards, and is a welcome addition to the bird-sounds in the garden. Four unmarked bluey-green eggs are laid in the neat nest of moss, grass and fibres. It lives in scrub, thickets and open woodland, throughout Britain. It is a resident species and one of our commoner birds.

WHITETHROAT

♀ ♂

GARDEN WARBLER

♀ ♂

BLACKCAP

BLACKCAP *(Sylvia atricapilla)* 14cm. To many people, the rich, varied warbling of the Blackcap is one of the loveliest bird songs of summer. Like other warblers, it is a migrant, but a hardy one, for in mild winters some individuals neglect to fly south for as long as they can find sufficient berries or insects. A bird of leafy lanes or woodland, the Blackcap sings as he moves about the branches, and is hard to see amongst the growing foliage. The males arrive a little earlier than the brown-capped females, and are in song by early April. It has a similar distribution to the Garden Warbler but is rather more widespread in Ireland.

WILLOW WARBLER *(Phylloscopus trochilus)* 11cm. One of our commonest and best-loved summer visitors, this little warbler has a huge breeding range across northern Europe and Asia. It is delicate both in form and plumage, and the sweet, rather sad, descending cadence of its song may be heard from every patch of scrub or woodland from early April until mid-July. The domed nest of grass is usually well concealed at, or very close to, ground level. Autumn birds, often abundant on passage, are much yellower than the pale spring birds.

CHIFFCHAFF *(Phylloscopus collybita)* 11cm. Although so similar in plumage to the Willow Warbler, you can distinguish this bird by its almost mechanical-sounding song of two repeated notes, from which it gets its name. It prefers tall trees and woods to scrub or commons, and often sings from a higher song-perch than the Willow Warbler. The nest is very similar, except that it is usually placed well above ground level. It is a common and widespread bird throughout Britain in summer, though absent from much of the Scottish highlands. In spring it is one of our earliest arrivals, the song often being heard before the end of March.

REED WARBLER *(Acrocephalus scirpaceus)* 12cm. ◁ Except when migrating, this little warbler is rarely found away from reed-beds, whether in a marsh or by a river or canal. A late arrival in spring, it is hard to see among the tall dead stems, although its rather monotonous chittering song gives it away. It is a great acrobat, and often perches with legs splayed wide apart as it grasps two stems, but on windy days the reed tops sway too much for comfort and it stays lower down. It is often the unwitting foster-parent for a young cuckoo, and the rather deep nest, which cuckoos seem able to find easily, is soundly woven round three or four reed stems.

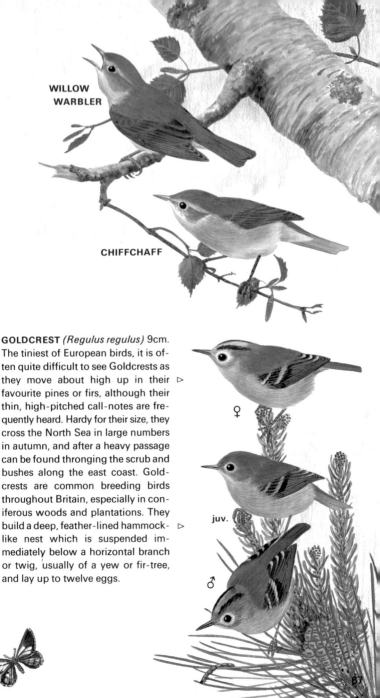

WILLOW WARBLER

CHIFFCHAFF

GOLDCREST *(Regulus regulus)* 9cm. The tiniest of European birds, it is often quite difficult to see Goldcrests as they move about high up in their ▷ favourite pines or firs, although their thin, high-pitched call-notes are frequently heard. Hardy for their size, they cross the North Sea in large numbers in autumn, and after a heavy passage can be found thronging the scrub and bushes along the east coast. Goldcrests are common breeding birds throughout Britain, especially in coniferous woods and plantations. They build a deep, feather-lined hammock- ▷ like nest which is suspended immediately below a horizontal branch or twig, usually of a yew or fir-tree, and lay up to twelve eggs.

♀

juv.

♂

♂ winter

PIED FLYCATCHER *(Ficedula hypoleuca)*
13cm. The cock bird in his pied summer
plumage is an attractive sight as he flutters
out from the fresh green of a birch in spring
after a passing fly. Flycatchers are summer
visitors, and this species nests in well-
wooded, often hilly, districts of Wales and
northern England, and parts of Scotland
and western England. It particularly likes
old oaks and birches, nesting in holes in the
trunks, and also takes easily to nest-boxes.
The males arrive several days before the
females and select the nest-hole, although
the female builds the nest on her own. They
are often conspicuous in eastern coastal
areas in autumn during the southerly
migration; at this time of year both old
males and young birds look like females.

SPOTTED FLYCATCHER *(Muscicapa stri-
ata)* 14cm. May is often a week old before
we notice that this quietly-plumaged flycatcher has arrived. Perched on a fence or
branch overlooking a clearing or lawn, the
upright stance and pale breast look un-
familiar at first, but the quick twisting flutter after a passing insect soon becomes an
accustomed feature of the garden. Indeed,
it is more accomplished at taking aerial
prey than its pied cousin. It nests in ivy, or
on a beam or branch, the young birds being
much more heavily spotted than their parents. It is a widespread breeding bird in
Britain, but is inclined to be solitary, even
when on migration.

STONECHAT *(Saxicola torquata)* 13cm. Open heathy or scrubby country-side and coastal areas are the home of these rotund little birds, whose white wing-patches catch the eye as they flutter down to the grass for insects. Stonechats like to sit on the tops of bushes and have a hard, chipping note (hence the name), so they are not difficult to find in the right places. Most of our Stonechats are resident, although there is some dispersal in winter, and some emigrate. It breeds regularly but rather locally throughout much of central and eastern England, but it is quite common elsewhere and is now increasing in numbers.
▽

WHEATEAR *(Oenanthe oenanthe)* 15cm. One of the earliest migrants to arrive in spring, when the male is a fine sight as he flits about the furrows of a newly-ploughed field. His plumage is noticeably greyer and more cleanly tinted in spring than in autumn, when buff and brown tints predominate, but at all times the flash of the white rump as the bird flies off is strik-ing. Any treeless country, whether moors, hills or dunes suits the Wheatear, and it is a conspicuous bird by the coast in autumn, when foreign-bred birds are passing through. The nest is often placed in a rabbit-burrow, or under a boulder on the ground. It is a common breeding bird in northern and western Britain, but in central and eastern England it tends to be re-stricted to preferred local areas.

♂

♀

♀

♂

WHEATEAR

△

REDSTART *(Phoenicurus phoenicurus)* 14cm. Spring has barely begun when the first Redstarts arrive from their winter home in Africa. The cock is one of the most attractive of the woodland or garden birds, with his constantly vibrating red tail, handsome plumage and sweet song. In courtship, the pairs chase through the woods, flirting their tails as they twist and turn, and the nest is built in a hole in a tree. It very rarely breeds in Ireland, but is widespread elsewhere and is commoner in the west and north.

BLACK REDSTART *(Phoenicurus ochruros)* 14cm. Common on rocky, open hillsides in much of Europe, it also likes to nest around buildings. It is a rare breeding bird in southern Britain, having first nested here 50 years ago in coastal cliffs, but now favours urban areas and industrial sites, derelict buildings and power stations. It is commoner as a passage migrant in autumn and spring, when many continental birds are moving to or from their winter quarters around the Mediterranean.

▽

ROBIN *(Erithacus rubecula)* 14cm. ▷
Although so friendly and appealing,
with his large dark eye, and head
cocked on one side, the Robin in pri-
vate life is very pugnacious. Much
territorial fighting occurs, both in the
spring and again in autumn when the
young birds are establishing their
own territories. It is interesting that
this bird, with its year-round pre-
occupation with territory, has developed two distinct songs, the
autumn one being sadder and more
wistful than the cheery warble of
summer. It is very widespread in
Britain, but is essentially a woodland
species with a liking for thick undergrowth, and does not feed in the open
too far from cover. The nest is often
well-concealed in a mossy stump or
bank, or in a shed, tree-hole or an old
tin, and is built by the hen only. Five or
six finely freckled eggs are laid, and
often two broods are reared. Our
Robins are mostly resident, although
there is much wandering in early
winter, and some may even cross the
Channel.

adult

imm.

71

adult

juv.

NIGHTINGALE *(Luscinia megarhynchos)* 16cm. The rich russet colour of the spread tail is often the only noticeable feature of the skulking Nightingale as it dives into deeper cover. It loves thick, tangled scrub and bushes, and is consequently a difficult bird to watch. It has a rather uniform brown plumage, and large dark eye, and in its actions the Nightingale is very similar to its close relative, the Robin. From late April onwards it pours out its richly vibrant and fluty song from a well-concealed perch near the ground and, contrary to much popular opinion, sings as much by day as it does by night. The period of song, however, is short, hardly lasting eight weeks. It is one of our later summer migrants to arrive and, although quite common where it does occur, is mainly confined as a breeding bird to England south of Yorkshire.

♀

♂
partly
albino

BLACKBIRD *(Turdus merula)* 25cm. An abundant resident throughout Britain, the Blackbird is for many people second only to the Nightingale as a songster, having a particularly mellow and fluty voice. It has a much shorter song period, though, than that other common garden songster, the Song Thrush, and is rarely heard before February or after July. A bird of woodland, gardens and town parks, it is also common in wilder countryside, even in small patches of bush on bleak hillsides or on the treeless northern isles. It is best adapted to living in thick cover, rarely feeding far out in the open, and uses its long tail to steer as it flies through the bushes, flicking it up for balance as it alights on a branch or fence. The female is sometimes confused with a thrush, but is darker and more uniform below; males often have white patches in the plumage, occasionally being all-white. British-bred Blackbirds are sedentary for the most part, their numbers being considerably swollen in winter by birds from the Continent.

♂

♀

73

SONG THRUSH

MISTLE THRUSH

MISTLE THRUSH *(Turdus viscivorus)* 27cm. This big thrush is an alert and wary bird, and likes to feed on fairly large open grassy areas such as parks or playing fields as well as pastureland. It holds itself erect, cocking its head as it listens for a worm, then hops off strongly for a yard or two to try another place. It often flies high, and shows the white corners of the tail as it swoops up to alight in a tree. It has a fine, wild song, and has earned the name "Stormcock" from its habit of singing on rainy, windy days in early spring. It is a resident species throughout Britain.

SONG THRUSH *(Turdus philomelos)* 23cm. A common bird in gardens, farms and woodland throughout Britain. The familiar song, in which each phrase is repeated several times, is among the best-known in town and countryside alike. On the ground the Song Thrush hops with legs well-flexed, flicking the dead leaves aside as it searches below the autumn hedgerows for insects or berries. It is fond of snails, and regularly uses the same brick or rockery stone as an anvil to break the shells. The nest is very commonly found in hedgerows and gardens, and is distinctive both for its smooth mud lining and for the four blue eggs that are laid in it.

REDWING

FIELDFARE

REDWING *(Turdus iliacus)* 21cm. Breeding in the birch and alder forests of northern Europe and Asia, the Redwing is a common winter visitor to countries further south. It has also nested in small but increasing numbers in northern Scotland over the last fifty years. From October onwards you will see it in the meadows and hedgerows in company with Fieldfares and Song Thrushes – look for its more striking head pattern, and the russet colour under the wing as it flies off. Rather surprisingly for such a northerly breeder, it is not a hardy bird, and many die if there is a prolonged cold spell after all the berries have been eaten.

FIELDFARE *(Turdus pilaris)* 25cm. This handsome, rather patchy-looking thrush is, like the Redwing, primarily a northern bird, although on the Continent it breeds as far south as Switzerland and France. There have also been a few breeding records in Britain in the last decade. The clear grey of the rump is striking as it flies away, and when a flock is passing high overhead the loud "chack-chack" call-notes are distinctive. It is a very gregarious bird, and you will often see it in large numbers in the winter in open countryside or in parks or playing fields. The flocks begin to thin out in March as the birds disperse northwards.

adult

COAL TIT

juv.

adult

BLUE TIT

GREAT TIT

adult

MARSH TIT

COAL TIT *(Parus ater)* 11cm. One of the few characteristic birds of coniferous woodland, the Coal Tit has benefited from the spread of plantations, and now nests in several areas where it was once unknown. In winter it searches through the trees with other tits, creepers and Redpolls, the white nape patch being easily visible when it hangs upside down from the tip of a twig. It has a thin, high-pitched call note, similar to a Goldcrest's note, and a song rather similar to the Great Tit's, only softer and sweeter.

GREAT TIT *(Parus major)* 14cm. The largest of the tits, it is an abundant bird throughout Britain. With the Blue Tit, its lively behaviour and readiness to come to a bird-table or use a nest-box make it one of our most popular birds. It has a distinctive "saw-sharpening" note sounding like "Teach-er", which is heard from February on, and a metallic call-note. It is just as acrobatic as the smaller tits, but tends to feed more about the trunk and larger branches than among the twigs, and often holds food such as nuts underfoot, while it picks out the contents.

BLUE TIT *(Parus caeruleus)* 11cm. A favourite visitor to most people's bird tables, the charming "Tom Tit" is fortunately very common and widely distributed. Its natural home is in deciduous woodland, especially oak. It is very vocal, and like other tits scolds harshly when upset, raising the brilliant azure crown feathers as it does so. It was the blue tit which learned to peck through milk-bottle tops in winter – a habit which has spread to other birds.

MARSH TIT *(Parus palustris)* 11cm. The name is a bit misleading; you are most likely to see one, or a pair, searching the branches in a wood or thicket, and they are not really as sociable as the other tits. It is an unobtrusive bird, but breeds quite commonly in England and Wales, although absent from Ireland and most of Scotland.

Tits and Nuthatches feeding together

northern form

WREN

△

LONGTAILED TIT *(Aegithalos caudatus)* 14cm. Unlike most tits, which nest in holes, this tiny and delightful bird makes one of the loveliest of all birds' nests – a dome of lichen and moss, deeply lined with feathers, and placed in a thick hedge, brambles or gorse. It is very sociable, many birds keeping company as they feed through a wood or along a hedge, flitting one after the other across the gaps, and keeping up a thin piping note. It is a resident bird, common in most of Britain, but is liable to be badly affected by hard winters. In northern European birds the head is all white.

WREN *(Troglodytes troglodytes)* 9.5cm. For such a small bird, the Wren's song, with its distinctive trills, is amazingly loud. It also has a churring or ticking alarm note. Rarely still, it creeps along a hedge or stone wall searching for insects, or flies low across the path, wings whirring. It sings, vibrating, with tail cocked jauntily, and wings drooped, and dashes headlong into cover if disturbed. The domed nest is tucked into an ivy-covered stump or bank. It is common throughout Britain.

NUTHATCH *(Sitta europea)* 14cm. The ▷
clear, repeated whistle of the Nuthatch is
a common sound of spring in parkland, or
in oak or beech woods. After a few minutes watching, you should be able to
make out the stumpy-tailed bird working
its way headfirst down a trunk, searching
for insects, or climbing about in the
branches to find nuts and seeds. It has
noticeably large feet and claws for a
small bird. It taps gently at the bark like a
miniature woodpecker. It nests in holes
and is very particular about the size of the
entrance, planting it up with mud until it
is just right. Although common in most
of England and Wales, it does not occur
in Scotland or Ireland.

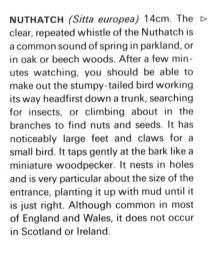

TREE-CREEPER *(Certhia familiaris)* ▷
13cm. At first sight, a Tree-creeper looks
rather mouse-like as it moves quietly up
the trunk of a big oak. It clings easily,
using its tail as a support, and spirals
round the trunk as it ascends, searching
the bark for insects. Once at the top, it flits
down to the base of another tree and
starts all over again. It has a rather thin,
Coal-tit like note, and you will often see
one keeping company with tits as they
search through the trees in winter. It
nests on a tree-trunk in a crack, or behind
a loose wedge of bark and, although
quiet and unassuming, is an active and
interesting bird to watch. It is common
throughout Britain.

YELLOWHAMMER

♂

♀

♀

♂

**CORN
BUNTING**

YELLOWHAMMER *(Emberiza citrinella)* 16cm. One of the most brightly coloured of our smaller birds, the cock Yellowhammer renders himself the more conspicuous by singing from an exposed perch on a hedge or bush. The familiar song is generally rendered as "A little bit of bread and no cheese". It is a resident bird, widely distributed in Britain in farmland, open country, gorsy commonland or along hedgerows. It is sociable in winter, forming flocks with Sparrows, Chaffinches and Greenfinches. It nests near the ground below a hedge or bush, and the eggs are covered with curious fine, scrawly lines.

CIRL BUNTING *(Emberiza cirlus)* 16cm. Looking very ▷ much like the Yellowhammer, the Cirl Bunting is confined to parts of Wales and south and west England, preferring more wooded country or tall trees along hedges. It can be distinguished by its dull olive, not chestnut, rump and in the male by the black throat.

◁ **REED BUNTING** *(Emberiza schoeniculus)* 14cm. Although typical of reed-beds and marshes, this bunting can also be found on moors or farmland, especially in winter. It likes to search through the tall dead vegetation by a ditch, or hops about close by, picking up seeds and constantly flicking its wings and tail. It often spreads the tail as it flies off, showing the white outer feathers. The cock clings to the swaying reed-heads as he sings his short, rattly song, and although handsome in his summer plumage, is duller and browner in winter. It is a resident bird throughout Britain.

CORN BUNTING *(Emberiza calandra)* 18cm. This large and heavily built bunting is rather dull and streaky, but can be told from females of other species by the lack of white in its tail. The male has a short, chirruping song, and sometimes dangles his legs in flight. Although common in some places, it is a rather local bird, occurring mostly in eastern, southern and central England and eastern Scotland. It frequents open country, farmland or coastal areas.

CHAFFINCH *(Fringilla coelebs)* 15cm. One of the commonest landbirds of Europe, and one of those birds whose song can sound quite different from one district to another. It is, like most finches, very sociable in winter, feeding in the woods or farmland with Greenfinches, Bramblings or other small birds. In summer it is a common breeding bird of gardens, parks and orchards – wherever in fact, there are bushes or trees to provide song-posts. The beautifully neat nest, made of grass and rootlets and decorated with moss and lichen, is placed in a hedge or small tree. Although they move about a good deal in winter our birds are resident, but their numbers are greatly increased in autumn by the arrival of continental-bred birds, many of which winter here.

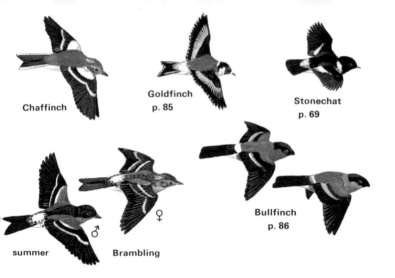

Chaffinch

Goldfinch
p. 85

Stonechat
p. 69

summer

♂

♀

Brambling

Bullfinch
p. 86

BRAMBLING *(Fringilla montifringilla)* 14cm. At a casual glance, a flock of Bramblings flying up from the woodland floor into the beeches might be mistaken for Chaffinches, but to a keen eye the brighter orange-buff patches and white rumps give them away. Winter visitors to Britain, they frequent woods, farmland or plantations, and feed to a great extent on beech-mast. The male in spring becomes very handsome, but by March or April the northward movement is under way, back to the breeding quarters in the Scandinavian forests.

♂
winter

CHAFFINCH

♂
winter

BRAMBLING

GREENFINCH *(Carduelis chloris)* 15cm. A stocky and short-tailed finch, whose rather dull-looking plumage as it feeds on the ground is enlivened by flashes of yellow on its wings and tail as it takes to the air. In summer the long nasal call can become monotonous, but the pleasant, conversational twittering is often heard from flocks as they feed amongst the weeds and stubble. As with many seed-eating finches, the young are fed mostly on insects. The nest is a loose structure of twigs and grass, often built in a garden hedge or evergreen tree. A resident bird found throughout Britain, it frequents mainly cultivated land or nearby woods and gardens.

SERIN *(Serinus serinus)* 11cm. This tiny, active and brightly coloured finch is spreading quite rapidly northwards from its traditional home. Several pioneer pairs have already nested in Britain. A sociable bird, it keeps mainly in the trees, where the male in spring sings his short, rattling song. He has also a pretty courtship flight, circling round with wings and tail outspread.

SISKIN *(Carduelis spinus)*
12cm. An attractive finch which seems to be on the increase. It breeds in spruce or mixed forests in Scotland and Ireland, but elsewhere is confined to a few selected areas. A great wanderer in winter, when parties can often be found feeding in alders. Siskins are very acrobatic, almost tit-like in their ability to swing upside-down amongst the twigs. They have recently taken to visiting bird-tables in Britain in winter, but are not always easy to see in the woods.

GOLDFINCH *(Carduelis carduelis)*
12cm. One of the most delightful of European birds. A party of Goldfinches, flitting through the swaying thistleheads, filling the air with their liquid twittering, is an enchanting sight, rich in life and colour. Not surprisingly, the Goldfinch became a favourite cagebird in the last century, and was trapped in large numbers. This, together with the spread of agriculture into its favourite areas of waste land, led to a decline in numbers. But it is now much commoner again and occurs throughout Britain, although less commonly in Scotland. It builds a beautiful, neat nest of fine rootlets and grass, lined with thistle-down and wool, and takes the seeds of many harmful farm and garden weeds.

adult

juv.

BULLFINCH *(Pyrrhula pyrrhula)* 15cm. One of the most retiring of our finches; often you will only catch a brief glimpse of the cock's bright colours and his white rump as he flies deeper into cover. Keeping closely to thickets, woodland or orchards, Bullfinches feed less on the ground than other finches, eating mostly buds, flowers and berries as well as weed-seeds. Unfortunately, a flock of Bullfinches can strip the young buds from a whole orchard in the space of a few hours and farmers regard them as pests. You will often see two together, and they are thought to pair for life, staying near their birthplace all their lives. Wanderings of more than a few miles are unusual. It is a widespread species throughout Britain.

LINNET *(Acanthis cannabina)* 13cm. A common and sociable little finch of gorsy commons, scrub, coastal saltings and wasteland. It occurs throughout Britain, and although there are Linnets here all year round, many of our home-bred birds spend the winter in southwest France, and their place here is taken by immigrants from the continent. Brown and streaky for most of the year, the cock becomes much brighter in the breeding season as the buff tips wear off his breast feathers to expose the crimson bases. Linnets make a charming sight as they feed among the weeds, clinging to the tall stems and twittering continually. Much white shows in the spread wings and tail.

TREE SPARROW *(Passer montanus)* 14cm. ▷
Slightly smaller and more cleanly marked
than its familiar cousin, the Tree Sparrow is
often overlooked, although the black cheek-
patch is obvious in both sexes. It is more a
bird of the countryside, living in small colonies in lines of pollarded willows or old
elms, nesting in the holes. In autumn and
winter it forages in the fields, often with
finches and buntings, and the flocks have a
distinctive short, hard flight call. A resident
species, it is common in England but rather
scarce in Ireland and northern Scotland.

HOUSE SPARROW *(Passer domesticus)*
15cm. A familiar bird of cultivated areas,
numerous around houses and town. Our two
species of sparrow are the only British representatives of the large tropical family of
weaver-birds – a relationship which is ap-
parent in the House Sparrow's domed nest
and colonial nesting habits. Its incessant
chirping and habit of eating spring flowers
make it rather a tiresome bird in the garden,
and when flocks feed in the ripening corn
they can do considerable damage. It is a
resident species throughout Britain although there is some immigration of continental birds in autumn.
▽

♂

♀

87

GOLDEN ORIOLE *(Oriolus oriolus)* 24cm. A rare visitor to southern and eastern England, occasionally staying to breed. The cock Oriole is one of the most lovely of European birds but, being a woodland dweller and rather shy, he is often difficult to see. The loud, fluty, triple whistle is a sure guide to the presence of an Oriole but, despite the brilliant colours, the bird is remarkably well camouflaged amongst the fresh green leaves and sun-dappled branches at the top of a tall oak or beech. The beautiful nest is slung like a little hammock below a branch. The Oriole is a summer visitor to most of Europe except Scandinavia, and winters in Africa.

winter

summer

Blackbird

STARLING *(Sturnus vulgaris)* 22cm. The beauty of the Starling's summer plumage is seldom appreciated, for the bird is so familiar that most people scarcely give it a second glance. The buff tips to the feathers which make it such a speckly bird in winter wear off in spring to reveal a purple and green-shot gloss worthy of a tropical sunbird. It is, despite its pushing ways, an interesting and successful species, and is highly sociable and adaptable. In winter the flocks are sometimes enormous, and their drop-pings befoul any wood or clump of rhododendrons used as a roost. In summer, they do some damage to soft fruit, but they more than make up for it by devouring huge quantities of harmful insects. The Starling has an extraordinary medley of whistles, squeaks and chattering noises, and adds to the effect by flapping its wings as it sits singing away on a chimney-pot. It is also an excellent mimic. Very widely distributed throughout the British Isles, most of our birds are sedentary, and more birds arrive here on a large scale from the continent in autumn.

Magpie

JAY *(Garrulus glandarius)* 34cm. This is the most brilliantly coloured of our crows. It is also the shiest and least easy to watch at close quarters. It is essentially a woodland bird, and often the only indication of its presence is a glimpse of the white rump, and a harsh squawk as it flies off deeper into cover. When out in the open, the flight looks laboured or even weak, and the wings look rather rounded. Like the Magpie it is an arch egg-thief and a menace to young birds, and is also partial to soft fruit, peas and beans, as any vegetable grower knows to his cost. Its chief natural diet, however, is beechmast, nuts and acorns, which are carried off and buried, a surprising number being found and eaten later. It is a widely distributed resident bird in Britain.

MAGPIE *(Pica pica)* 46cm. Because of its preference for more open or lightly wooded country, and its bold plumage pattern, this is a more conspicuous bird than the Jay. Magpies especially like to sit on the top of a tree or tall hedge where they can survey the surrounding countryside, and no doubt locate nests which they can plunder. Their harsh chatter is a familiar sound, and in early spring they gather in noisy, active parties in which there is much posturing and displaying. Like all crows, it is a wary bird, and shares the family habit of stealing bright or shiny objects, which it hoards. The domed nest of twigs is quite often a conspicuous object in a sparsely foliaged hedge or tree.

JAY

MAGPIE

ROOK

HOODED CROW

CARRION CROW

JACKDAW

92

ROOK *(Corvus frugilegus)* 46cm. One of the most characteristic features of farmland bird-life is the flocks of Rooks feeding in the fields, or the long, straggling lines flapping back to the rookery in the evenings. Highly sociable, the Rook is our largest really common land-bird, although its numbers have declined in recent years, possibly due to the widespread use of poisonous seed-dressings. A resident bird, its numbers are swelled in autumn by the arrival of continental birds which spend the winter here. Young rooks lack the bare white skin at the base of the bill.

CARRION CROW *(Corvus corone)* 47cm. Much less regularly seen in flocks than the Rook, the Carrion Crow is decidedly non-sociable, the individual pairs being well scattered around the countryside. It is an adaptable, wary and voracious bird, and has long been high on the list of "vermin" to be shot by gamekeepers. It is an aggressive menace to smaller birds when they are nesting, ruthlessly robbing them of eggs and chicks. It occurs throughout England, Wales and southern Scotland, being common in coastal areas, and is also surprisingly frequent in towns and parks.

The **Hooded Crow** in its most typical plumage is easy to tell from the Carrion Crow, although both birds are in fact races of the same species, and interbreed over large areas of Europe and Asia. The "Hoodie" is the common form in north and west Scotland and Ireland, and you may see immigrants from the continent in eastern coastal areas of England in winter.

JACKDAW *(Corvus monedula)* 33cm. Our only other really gregarious crow, it is smaller and more compact than the Rook, and flies with quicker wing-beats. Jackdaws flock around coastal cliffs, old buildings and churches, and in parks with old timber, nesting in holes in trees or masonry. They feed in nearby fields, often consorting with Rooks and Starlings, and when on the ground the white eye and grey back to the head and neck are easily seen. It is a common resident species throughout Britain, with arrivals from the continent increasing their numbers in winter.

Index of English Names

Index of Scientific Names